MW00879406

What Do You Know About Dance?

Guide for Parents

And Young Dancers

ANASTASIIA OHIRCHUK

Copyright © 2024 Anastasiia Ohirchuk

All rights reserved.

ISBN: 9798327131637

DEDICATION

This book is dedicated to all those who believe in the magic of movement, who is certain of the fact that dance can bestow expression and sensation. From parents who support their children on their dance journey to every dancer who pours his/her heart out on the stage. May this book be your gateway to the world of dance diversity, helping you understand its history, lesson structures, style choices, and inspiring you to achieve your dance goals.

With love, Anastasiia Ohirchuk

CONTENTS

ACKNOWLEDGMENTS

I extend my heartfelt gratitude to everyone who contributed to the creation of this book. From the tireless research and writing process to the countless conversations with dancers, instructors, and parents, this project would not have been possible without your support.

Special thanks to my dance mentors, whose wisdom and passion have shaped my understanding of movement and choreography. Honored Culture Worker of Ukraine, Associate Professor Larysa Tsvetkova, who showed me the ballet dance from a completely different point of view. Candidate of Art Criticism, Associate Professor Victor Lytvynenko, who discovered for me the essence of the choreographic performances. Doctor of Arts, Professor Alina Pidlypska, who taught me to express choreographic thoughts on a paper. And Aniko Rekhviashvili, who were National Artist, Ballet Master and Artistic Director of National Ukrainian Opera Ballet, who taught me to think outside the box and express my thoughts within the dance.

I am indebted to my family for their unwavering encouragement and belief in my vision. My mother, Iryna Chvarkova, who decided, at all costs, that I should dance. My sister and my best friend, Alona Kindyk, proofread my countless drafts and was my greatest support and helper. My husband and my son, Volodymyr & Oleksandr Ohirchuk, attended my every recital, cheering from the front row. Your love and enthusiasm have fueled my determination to bring this book to life.

Lastly, to the readers – whether you're a beginner dancer, a curious parent, or someone exploring the world of dance for the first time – thank you for embarking on this journey with me. May these pages inspire, inform, and ignite your own dance aspirations.

With immense appreciation,

Anastasiia Ohirchuk

INTRODUCTION

My name is Anastasiia Ohirchuk.

My first encounter with the dance occurred in the distant 1996, or was it 1997, when I was around 4-5 years old. I was a clumsy little girl, and my mother, worrying about me, decided to enroll me in the dance classes. Of course, I had no idea about the vast array of the dance styles and their complexities. To me, dancing seemed like a fun and active pastime.

That's what my feet looked like (Pre-K, 1996)

AI Picture (Dance Room)

We entered a beautiful studio adorned with floor-to-ceiling mirrors. Alongside these mirrors were poles that I did not quite understand at the time (now I can confidently say they were dance barres, which dancers use to learn and practice specific movements). The children around me were dressed in lovely outfits. The younger dancers wore ballet slippers on their feet, while the older ones had peculiar shoes with square, rigid toes (pointe shoes) tied elegantly around their legs.

For some time, my mother has been talking with an elegantly dressed woman who shot me a quick and cold glance before approaching. She began positioning me, like I was a little soldier, sometimes gathering my legs together, other times lifting them one by one. Then she uttered a chilly "NO". That "No" was as scorching as her gaze. I didn't know what it meant, but I felt hurt and bewildered... Was I worse than others?

That was my brief and intense introduction to classical dance (Ballet Dance).

Driven by an unwavering desire to align my legs at all costs, my mother's next destination became Dances of Different World Nationalities or Folk Choreography. I was welcomed into the dance group classes without trials. From that moment on, the dance won my heart. It was love at second sight.

Describing my entire dance history doesn't make much sense here, as I'd like to include more educational information in this book. However, it's worth to mention that at this point I haven't stopped searching for the best dancing experience...

I was born in a fairly poor family. My parents borrowed money from people every month and used their entire salary to repay those debts. The 1990s were a difficult time, with an economic crisis and the collapse of the Soviet Union, which likely influenced the events.

Naturally, inflation was rising, and prices increased, including those for children's activities like dance classes. As a result, my folk dance lessons became quite expensive for my family, and I had to quit.

Of course, like any other mother, my mom couldn't leave her child without a beloved activity. So, we embarked on a new search.

Here, on my path, I encountered a class of "Ballroom Dance". It was impossible to look away from the dancing couples in their vibrant attire. It was captivating. But this type of dance turned out to be much more expensive that the previous ones...

The next stop was called "Folk Choreography" again – where I practiced until completing my high school. Significant achievements were made during my time there, leading to a recommendation to join a semi-professional ensemble affiliated with the Ukrainian National University. It was time when I received my first paycheck for the performance, dancing with this ensemble.

The logical continuation of my entire choreographic journey was pursuing higher education at the Kyiv National University of Culture and Arts, studying full-time on a budget basis, and receiving a Master's Degree in Choreography. During this period, I wrote my first research paper titled "Theatre Directing Aspects of Ballet Master Activity in Folk Choreography", which was presented at the All-Ukrainian Scientific and Practical Conference in 2016 and published in the book "Choreography of the 21st Century: Artistic and Educational Potential".

First research paper

Master's Diploma

Next, I delved into my extensive experience in choreography and rapid career growth. I transitioned from a Dance Instructor to the Chief Choreographer at the Philharmonic. I have conducted a large number of master classes in various choreographic styles and have been involved in creative productions as an invited Choreographer and Ballet Master in theaters and ensembles around the country and beyond.

Today, I continue to promote and glorify choreography in all its aspects in the United States. I also strive to improve my level of qualifications and knowledge. As a result, I have received a certificate from Harvard University upon completion of the course "Stravinsky's Rite of Spring: Modernism, Ballet, and Riots", and a certificate from Emory University for the course "So You Think You Know Tango".

So, why do you need to read this book?

• This book unveils the enchanting world of dance – the history behind each step, the emotions conveyed through movements, and the transformative power of rhythm.

• Explore dance diversity from ballet to ballroom, modern to folk, this book celebrates the rich tapestry of dance styles. Readers can explore different genres, learn about their origins, and appreciate uniqueness of each form.

• An overview of different types of choreography, each with its own pros and cons (of course, this is a subjective opinion).

• An explanation of what is the history of creation of each type of choreography and its structure.

• An examination of how each dance direction defines the dancer's appearance, skills, and engagement of specific muscle groups.

• Whether young dancers dreaming of the stage or professional performers seeking fresh inspiration, this book encourages to embrace your dance aspirations.

• Dive into the historical context of dance – from its ancient origins to contemporary trends. This book sheds light on the evolution of dance, making it a valuable resource for both novices and seasoned dance enthusiasts.

• Reading about the dance sparks creativity. It encourages readers to express themselves through movement, whether they're twirling in a studio or simply tapping their feet to the beat.

If you're holding this book in your hands, then surely my work is something that can answer your questions and solve your problems in choosing the dance type for yourself or your little one. Let's dive into each of the choreographic directions!

1 TYPES OF CHOREOGRAPHY

When it comes to choreography or dance, I believe we can all agree that "movement is life". Indeed, dance does not only enhance physical health but also positively impacts the joints, heart, and circulatory system by evenly engaging all muscle groups. But that's not all:

1. **Emotional Well-being**: Dancing allows the expression and release of the emotions.
2. **Musical Aptitude**: It sharpens your musical ear and sense of rhythm.
3. **Social Skills**: Dance fosters communication, and aesthetic development.
4. **Coordination and Artistry**: It refines coordination and artistic expression.
5. **Social adaptation**: Each and every dance shapes a person's taste for music, clothes, behavior etc.
6. **Intellect**: Yes, dance even influences intelligence! As it helps you to orient yourself in time and space, it cultivates resilience, independence, persistence, initiative, and more.

So, the next time you hit the dance floor, know that you're not just moving your body – you're nurturing your mind and soul as well!

The benefits of dance in everyone's life are immense. Let's start with my example: my feet are slender and straight, and of course, I have no more clumsiness. I walk confidently, without worrying about tripping over my own feet. But on a more serious note, dance contributes to proper posture, a well-proportioned figure, and muscle strength.

Before we proceed further, I'd like to highlight a few historical facts.

Dance has been an integral part of human history since its earliest origins, transcending spiritual rituals and creating bonds within communities. For instance:

AI Picture.

• In India, prehistoric cave paintings dating back to approximately 8000 BCE depict early dance.

• Egyptian tomb paintings, around 3300 BCE, also showcase dance. These early dances may have had religious significance.

AI Picture.

• By the era of ancient Greece, people incorporated dance into celebrations of the wine God Dionysus (later the Roman God Bacchus) and ritual dances at the ancient Greek Olympic Games.

AI Picture.

Dance served as a means of social communication and bonding. In summary, dance's impact extends beyond physical movement – it connects us culturally, emotionally, and spiritually.

So, when it comes to "what dance give us", I believe there won't be any disagreements. But when it comes to varieties and styles of dance, let's consider a following scenario: Imagine gathering ten different people who don't know each other and haven't interacted before. Some of them might have danced or still dancing, while others have dedicated their lives to IT technologies and have never even thought about dancing. Now, let's ask them: "What types of dance do you know?" Here's where the immense surprise comes in – you'll hear an unbelievable number of answers, and all of them will be correct.

Nowadays, choreography is rapidly evolving, giving rise to many new branches – from modern choreography to contemporary, from street dance to avant-garde. However, among these respondents, there will undoubtedly be common answers, such as "classical dance or ballet, ballroom choreography, folk dance, and hip-hop or modern dance".

I propose hunt through the fundamental forms of choreography, their history, and structure. And, as far as possible, try to understand where the new dance styles came from and why it happened.

2 CLASSICAL DANCE OR BALLET

I intentionally begin with an overview of classical dance because I believe it serves as the foundation of all dance forms.

2.1 A BRIEF HISTORY OF CLASSICAL DANCE/BALLET

We already know or have previously learned that dance is one of the oldest forms of art. The development of this art has gone through several stages, developing alongside society. Historians speculate that dance movements were used by early humans even before the advent of speech. They could convey emotions and experiences to one another with the help of dance.

In medieval Europe, with the arrival of Christianity, dance was considered a relic of the pagan past. Ritualistic dance nearly disappeared, and even folk dance lost its favor. However, in the 14th century, courtly dances (such as the Branle, Sardana, Pavane and so on) gained popularity among the nobility. These are now known as historical social dances. Court balls became fashionable.

AI Picture.

Finally, in the 17th century, ballet emerged. The first ballet school opened, and the profession of dance master (choreographer) came into existence. Imagine the centuries of evolution that led to this point! So, classical dance not only reflects artistic expression but also carries the weight of cultural and historical significance.

Let's remember this prehistory; it will come in handy as we discuss ballroom choreography.

Interestingly, if we ask the question: "Where and when did ballet originate?" – the answers from different sources vary. Some might say "It originated in Italy", others would claim France, and still others attribute the entire history of ballet to Russia.

And, in my opinion, it's all true. Because in Italy, ballet existed at aristocratic courts. This was during the Renaissance period. Perhaps Domenico de Ferrara, who wrote the work "De arte saltandi et choreus ducendi" (about the art of dance and its introduction), was the most renowned choreographer. Or perhaps records of other choreographers from that era simply haven't survived...

When Catherine de Medici (an Italian aristocrat) married Henry II (heir to the French throne), she brought Italian courtly dance to France. Perhaps the first ballet could be considered the "Comedy Ballet of the Queen" (1581), choreographed by Balthazar de Beaujoyeulx. It lasted 5 hours and included dances, dialogues, and dramatic elements.

In the same year, Italy was recognized as a center for the development of dance technique.

In 1588, the first French book about dance, titled "Orchesographie", was published by Thoinot Arbeau. It even mentioned intricacies of dance steps.

Than, in 1661, the world's first ballet school, the "Royal Academy of Dance", was established in France by Louis XIV. Later on, that school became known as the "Paris Opera Ballet".

Paris. France. Royal Academy of Dance.

9

Interestingly, if we examine the widely accepted terminology of classical dance, we'll notice that it is predominantly in French, rather than Italian.

From the mid-1730s onward, England saw an increased focus on ballet. English choreographer John Weaver created ballet d'action (ballet without spoken words). Opera theaters started opening across Europe, and dancers and instructors easily found employment.

But why do many people consider Russia to be the "birthplace" of classical dance?

During a time when ballet was waning in Europe (around 1850), it thrived in Russia thanked to skilled masters: August Bournonville, Jules Perrot, Arthur Saint-Leon, Enrico Cecchetti, and Marius Petipa. Fun fact is that none of them were born in Russia; they brought the development of classical choreography to the stages of St. Petersburg. And within the Imperial Russian Ballet they created iconic performances: Marius Petipa's "Don Quixote" (1869), Petipa's "La Bayadere" (1877), "Swan Lake" (originally choreographed by Venzel Ratzinger and later revised by Joseph Hansen and Marius Petipa in 1895), and "The Nutcraker" (Petipa and Lev Ivanov).

In the 1890s, balled stopped being a major art form in Western Europe and didn't exist in America. Only three individuals from Russia rekindled interest in ballet: Enrico Cecchetti, Sergei Diaghilev, and Agrippina Vaganova.

Enrico Cecchetti (1850-1928).
Pic was taken from Wikipedia.
He was an Italian ballet dancer, a choreographer, and a teacher. Enrico made significant contributions to the world of ballet, a rigorous and systematic approach to ballet training. His method emphasizes precise placement, alignment, and coordination.

Sergei Diaghilev (1872-1929).
Pic was taken from Wikipedia.
He was a Russian arts promoter who revitalized ballet by integrating the ideals of other art forms – music, painting, and drama – with those of dance.

Agrippina Vaganova (1879-1951).
Pic was taken from Wikipedia.
She was a Russian ballerina, a choreographer, and a teacher who made significant contributions to the world of ballet. Vaganova's method became the foundation for all Soviet ballet trainings. Her efforts ensured the survival of Russian ballet and expanded its impact on other dance styles. Her legacy continues to shape ballet education worldwide.

The history of ballet dance is a vast topic. There were numerous achievements and discoveries, such as the emergence of pointe work (when the ballerinas start dancing on the tips of the toes) and more. Costumes evolved from heavy and cumbersome to lightweight. Changes occurred in dance roles; initially, female roles did not exist in classical dance masterpieces. But there also were lots of masterpieces of ballet dance which endure even nowadays without any changes.

Ballet "Don Quixote".
Mariinsky Theater.
Choreography by Alexander Gorsky (1902).
Based on the ballet by Marius Petipa.

Classical ballet by Marius Petipa "La Bayadere". Music by Ludwig Mincus.
Brilliant Classical Stanislavsky Ballet and Opera Theater.

2.2 MODERN STRUCTURE OF CLASSICAL DANCE

In the present day, a classical dance school primarily emphasizes hard work, and a clear understanding of the art form. Having come a long way in its development, ballet now has precise definitions, terminology, and a structured framework.

Here's how it typically unfolds:

1.   *Introduction for Young Dancers (Ages 3 to 5)*:

• Young dancers often begin their journey with rhythmic exercises (movements accompanied by music that instill a sense of rhythm and auditory awareness).

• They also engage in stretching or floor exercises to enhance muscle flexibility and strength.

2.   *Intermediate and Advanced Levels*:

• Older students focus on refining their performance technique within a structured class format.

• The class structure typically revolves around three components:

■ *Exercises* – these are performed at the ballet barre or in the center of the studio hall.

■ *Allegro* – this refers to jumps and various types of leaps.

■ *Adagio* – it emphasizes stability, free control of the torso, expressive arm movements, and overall technical proficiency.

Let's explore each of these components and delve into some French terminology (since we know that ballet terminology is predominantly in French).

Exercises: These are a series of movements aimed at developing flexibility, turnout of the legs, and strengthening the musculoskeletal system. Exercise can be performed both at the ballet barre and it the center of the studio hall, alternating legs. The sequence remains consistent, except for variations as dancers progress in their trainings.

Certainly! Let's now speak about the terminology of the classical structure of exercises:

1. ***Demi and Grand Plié [dem'ɪ: plɪ'e]:*** These movements develop leg strength and turnout, as well as flexibility in the hip, knee, and ankle joints.

2. ***Battement Tendu ['batmənt tɒn'd(j)uː]:*** It develops knee extension, foot pointing, and overall leg strength.

3. ***Battement Tendu Jeté ['batmənt tɒn'd(j)uː ʒeté]:*** This step emphasized lightness and agility in the hip joint and prepares the feet for jumps.

4. ***Rond de Jambe Par Terre [rɒnd də ʒam par terʃ]:*** It enhances rotational mobility of the hip joint.

5. ***Battement Fondu ['batmənt fən'd(j)uː]:*** This step develops leg strength and ligament elasticity.

6. ***Battement Frappé ['batmənt fra'pe]:*** It promotes knee agility and quickness.

7. ***Rond de Jambe en L'air [rɒnd də ʒam ən lǽr]:*** This movement focuses on knee mobility.

8. ***Petit Battement [pu: 'batmənt]:*** It is a free possession of the lower part of the leg from knee to foot.

9. ***Battement Développé and/or Battement Relevé Lent ['batmənt ‚dıvelop'e ǽnd/v: 'batmənt rele've lan]:*** These steps develop leg stretching (like a high kick or split) and the necessary strength for jumping.

10. ***Grand Battement Jeté [gran 'batmənt ʒeté]:*** It further develops leg stretching and contributes to inner hip muscles and tendons development, intensifying hip joint work.

Feel free to explore these terms further – they're the basics for classical dance!

The next part of the lesson is ***Allegro.*** It's the most challenging yet expressive aspect of classical dance – jumps. The technique of a jump involves propulsion, elevation, and landing or completion. In ballet, there are various groups of jumps:

○ Two Feet to Two Feet: Jumping from both feet and landing on both feet.
○ Two Feet to One Foot: Jumping from both feet and landing on one foot.
○ One Foot to Two Feet: Jumping from one foot and landing on both feet.
○ One Foot to the Other Foot: Jumping from one foot and landing on the other foot.
○ On One Foot: Jumping from and landing on the same foot.

These groups define the starting position from which the jump is executed and the final position where the dancer lands.

Jumps can be categorized into small (where high elevation is not necessary), medium, and large (where elevation matters).

Allegro consists of *Changement de Pied*, *Petit Pas Assemble*, *Double Assemble*, *Petit Pas Jete*, *Pas Glissade*, *Pas Chasse*, *Pas de Chat*, *Pas de Basque*, various types of *Sissonnes*, and more complex forms, as well as combinations of different jumps.

Adagio is a part of dance consisting of various types of *Developpe*, slow turns in *Tour Lent* positions, *Port de Bras*, various *Renverse* movements, *Grand Fouette*, *Tour Sur le Cou-de-Pied*, and turns in large positions.

This section of the lesson holds immense significance. As adagio is a whole part of the dance, it's not just one movement. It unites a series of movements into one harmonious whole. Interestingly, in male stage dance (in contrast to female), adagio as a dance form is not encountered. However, its study is equally essential for both female and male classes because it is closely linked to jumps, especially the grand ones, and imparts them proper form.

And now it's clear why my mother chose a classical dance school for me. And despite the fact that I wasn't accepted there, ballet dance was a great part of my experience in folk choreography. We'll discuss further ballet in "Folk Choreography" chapter.

2.3 CLASSICAL DANCE PERFORMER'S LOOK

The attire for classical dance is a crucial element in preparing for proper dance technique. Yes, that's right – uniform is intricately connected to the correct execution of movements. Why? It's quite simple.

Tight-fitting leotards allow the classical dance instructor to notice and correct the performer's mistakes. Soft shoes (such as ballet slippers) facilitate free movement and development of footwork. Here, I'd like to emphasize ballet slippers, not other ballet shoes. Often, they are mistakenly considered the same. Unlike ballet shoes, ballet slippers are made of fabric and have leather sole which look like two separate parts with a fabric arch in between them, allowing the shoe to fit snugly on the dancer's foot while maintaining foot mobility. In contrast, ballet shoes are relatively rigid footwear made entirely of leather. Personally, I find a ballet shoe looks like a fin, limiting foot full functionality.

Ballet slippers.   Other ballet shoes.

Additional attire element can include a chiffon skirt (for girls) and pointe shoes (footwear designed for dancing on the tips of the toes, typically for older female dancers).

Pointe shoes (AI picture).

Uniform for classical dance.

Hair should be neatly pulled back into a tight bun. The forehead should be exposed, which means the bangs are also tucked away. Untidily arranged hair can be distracting, obstructive, and even cause harm (such as getting into your eyes or your partner's eyes during turns, etc.).

It's worth mentioning that stage costumes differ from dance attire because they must align with the conceptual content.

Classical dance serves as the foundation of choreography. While there are numerous contemporary dance styles today, they all trace their origins back to ballet dance.

3 FOLK DANCE OR DANCES OF DIFFERENT WORLD NATIONALITIES

Folk dance holds a special place in my life. Not only because it is the dance that won the battle in the fight called "My clumsiness or how to fight it", but also because it instilled in me a love for choreography that has lasted my entire life. This is the choreography that opened the whole world for me, showing how different mentalities and cultures can be. Believe me, at that time, which was the end of the 90s, it was almost impossible to leave the countries of the former Soviet Union. And no one dared to think about it, even having money for traveling. What is unknown is always scary. Now I smile when I think about that time... After all, today anyone with a desire can visit any country just by buying a flight ticket. Well, look at me, I am writing this book now sitting at my cozy home in the United States of America.

But let's get back to folk choreography.

3.1 HISTORY OF FOLK DANCE

The term "folk dance" is applied to dances that have historical significance. Sometimes you can come across terms like "ethnic dance" or "traditional dance". M. V. Gogol (novelist and playwrite of Ukrainian origin), gave a concise characteristic to folk dance in his "Petersburg Notes" of 1836: "Look, folk dance appear in different corners of the world: a Spaniard does not dance like a Swiss, a Scot does not dance like a German, a Russian does not dance like a

Frenchman or an Asian. Even in the provinces within the same state, the dance changes."

Characteristic features of different cultures began to form in the distant past. The first dances arose as a manifestation of emotional impressions from the surrounding world. All important events in the life of an early human being – birth, death, the choice of a new tribal leader, prayer for a harvest or good weather – were accompanied with the dance. Choreography art is an integral part of any human community, in any ethnographic group.

AI Picture.

Over time, choreography changed, and each ethnic group developed its own features. In Ancient Egypt, the art of dance was predominantly ceremonial. In Antiquity, militarized dances were added to the ceremonial dances, which were designed to raise the spirit of warriors before a battle. In Ancient Greece, with the development of theatrical art, stage dance also appeared. In the Middle Ages, there was a division into court and village dances. This division did not yet have clear boundaries, and often the same movements were present both at the courts and in folklore. At some point at this stage, classical dance and folk dance separated and continued their formations separately from each other.

And here we come to the question that torments my soul. Which dance was first, folk or ballet? I have studied the history of dance very carefully from the origins. And of course, the concise answer would be "folk dance", as this term can boldly award the first performances of dance in general. But, if you delve deeper and start analyzing both dance types of choreography at the moment, I mean analyzing them as structured dances as they are nowadays. Then you can trace the regularity of the formation of folk dance based on classical dance. This means that the formation of ballet dance happened earlier.

The oldest type of folk dance, which exists in almost all ethnographic groups, is the round dance. Its movements are simple and consist of walking in a circle, accompanied with the music or singing. Most likely, the form of a circle symbolized the sun. The round dance still exists among all Slavic nations. In Lithuania, it is called Korogod, in Moldova – Hora, in Ukraine – Khorovod, in Bulgaria and Romania – Horo, among Croats and Bohemians – Kolo.

AI Picture.

Each folk dance is an essential part of the national culture of each country. There are countless styles and types of folk dances, but they all have one thing in common – they reflect the chronology of every national history, its soul and character.

Folk dance is a wonderful opportunity to visit any spot on the globe without leaving the dance hall.

3.2 ETHNICITIES AND THEIR CHOREOGRAPHIC COLOR

Have you ever wondered how many countries exist in the world? According to Wikipedia, at the moment, the United Nations includes 193 countries and 2 non-member observer states – Vatican City State or the Holy See and Palestine State. Additionally there are approximately ten countries, which are actually independent, but either are not recognized by other countries, or are recognized by an insufficient number of them. The International Olympic Committee, at the same time, records 206 independent countries.

If you imagine that each country has its own national dance, then you can simply count that in our world, as of today, there are at least 206 different folk dances with their own culture of performance. Of course, this is doubtful, because we know that even in different regions of one country there are different varieties of folk choreography; that is, one country can have more than a dozen folk dances.

Listing all the folk dances and their features is impossible, my whole life wouldn't be enough to describe them all. This is despite the fact that a fairly large number of folk dances are unknown to me. For instance, thinking of the tribes that inhabit our earth today or those small countries, the existence of which we have not even heard.

Nevertheless, with your permission, I would like to mention the most vivid folk dances of our days (this is my subjective point of view).

Ukraine: Of course, I want to start with the country, which is my Motherland and its folk dance called *"Hopak".* For some reason, I think that this dance is known to great number of people. It is very bright, colorful, and picturesque. The "Hopak" dance includes the combat skills of Ukrainian Cossacks, so it was originally performed exclusively by men. Later on, women added color to this dance, emphasizing the courage, strength, and agility of the partners. This choreography is filled with a huge amount of virtuoso technique, such as: *obertas, shine* (one of the turn types), *pike, splits* (split in a jump performed by men), *crawl, barrel,* and much more.

It is believed that the men's costumes used for Hopak dance (red trousers, embroidered shirt, and boots) are, in essence, the uniform of the Cossacks of that time; and women's costumes (embroidered shirt, skirt, corset, boots, and wreath with ribbons) – historical clothing of Ukrainian women.

P. Virsky Ukrainian National Folk Dance Ensemble.

Ireland: "Ceili" is a general term for all Irish dances, which originated from the ancient ceremonial dances of Ireland and Scotland. These dances are based, practically, on the same movements: on high half-fingers with special steps (jumps) forming various figures from 30 schemes or dancing separate elements in place. Great attention is paid to the coordination of dancers, synchronization of their performance, agility, tirelessness, and sense of rhythm.

It should be noted that Irish Ceili dance is performed by women wearing only soft shoes (ghilies), men wear harder shoes, similar to tap shoes, which make distinctive sounds when tapping feet. Traditional Irish dance costumes reflect the rich history and cultural heritage of Ireland, combining elements of Gaelic history with modern trends: bright women's dresses with traditional Irish patterns (Celtic knots, spirals, shamrocks), men's black or dark green trousers, shirt, vest, jacket. Sometimes, the male costume is complemented by an Irish plaid, which is worn over the shoulder.

Greece: "Sirtaki" does not have a centuries-old history, although this dance contains elements of Greek dance styles, in particular – *syrtos, pidikhtos,* and *hasapiko* (an ancient dance of warriors). At first, the movements are slow, and then they accelerate. "Sirtaki" itself becomes incredibly energetic and lively. All performers hold hands or put them on each other's shoulders.

It is noteworthy that in 2012 this dance entered the Guinness Book of Records for the most numerous performance (5164 people).

In this dance, various outfit options can be used. Greek national costumes are characterized by a wealth of colors and ornamentation. Men: wide-step trousers with narrow legs (vraka), belt, pharaoh (feska) or turban, short jacket, short skirt (fustanella). Women: tunic-like shirt with a long wide skirt (fusta), apron, and belt.

Greek Night in Rhodes Town (2023).

Gypsy dance is considered one of the most beautiful. This is explained by incredible movements with large leg throws, body bends, rhythm beats, and turns. Also, the costumes of the dancers, which include women's long colorful skirts ('two suns') and tap dance shoes for men.

In gypsy dance, it is possible to use a drum or shawl. A distinctive feature is the manner of performance – gypsy character, inner freedom, and audacity.

For a long time, it was believed that the homeland of the Gypsies is Egypt, until in 1855 the German academic August Friedrich Pott proved their Indian origin. He found the direct ancestors of modern Gypsies in Ancient India, who are now scattered all over the world.

Spain: The dance ***"Flamenco"*** originates from the Spanish province of Andalusia, which was originally presented with percussion, "flying" hands, and expressive singing under the guitar and castanets. The adventurous character of the Spaniards could not resist the music of the wind and dramatic singing. They came up with special steps: they beat the rhythm with sharp heels, clicked their fingers, clapped the rhythm with their hands (palmas), led a sharp and extremely expressive hand game, shouted "Ole" as a result of which a passionate dance was born, which is called "fiery".

Bata de cola – a traditional women's dress for Flamenco dance, the shape of which resembles the dresses of gypsies. On top of the dress, dancers wear a shawl, sometimes they tie it around the waist to emphasize grace. The male costume – dark trousers with

25

a wide belt and shirt. Sometimes a red scarf is tied around the neck.

India: The traditional national dance of India is ***"Bharatanatyam"*** (bhava – feelings, emotions; raga – melody; talam – the art of rhythm; natyam – dance). Originally, this dance had a sacred meaning, which is confirmed by various poses of Bharatanatyam carved on the walls of temples in South India. In addition to the dance itself, it includes abhinaya (the art of mime). Using the language of gestures, the performer can express their emotions and tell a certain story. The technique of modern dance performance includes 9 states/moods: love, disgust, heroism, fear, joy, sadness, surprise, anger, and peace. A distinctive feature of the style is the emphasized geometry of poses, symmetry of the dance pattern, sharp and precise movements, and deliberate conventionality of mime and gestures.

The traditional dance attire for women is a sari or ghagra-choli – a long piece of dyed fabric, has beautiful patterns; and bindi – part of women's makeup. Traditional clothing for men is sherwani (long overcoat), kurta (loose long shirt), and dhoti (resembles short trousers) or lungi.

Italy: The dance ***"Tarantella"*** is believed to have originated from dances of people bitten by a spider. It is one of the bright national symbols of Italy. Tarantella in its structure is a fairly fast and synchronous dance. Tempo, rhythm, and elements of improvisation are equally important in it. Distinctive movements include changing the frontal position to circular, constant movements, alternations, and repetitions. The movements of the dancers are springy, with an accent on each step. Hand movements complement wrist rotations.

The variety of folk costumes in Italy unites brightness and colorfulness. The main elements of the female costume: camichia (tunic-like shirt), gonna (wide pleated skirt), corsetto (corset), grembiule (apron), fracciletto (headscarf). Men's costume: pantaloni (short trousers), embroidered shirt, giacca (short jacket), and hat.

And of course, I simply must not fail to mention **America**, where I currently reside.

I have been studying for a long period of time and continue to study the dance culture of America with great persistence. For me, this is not an easy topic. USA is the country that was formed in 1776, which means that it will turn 248 years old this year (2024). And if you take into account the War of Independence, which ended in 1783, then the number of years for the creation of national authenticity will decrease to 241. Since the United States is the homeland for people of many races and ethnic groups, it becomes even more difficult to find a national flavor.

For a long time, I considered *"Country"* to be the national dance of USA. But is this correct? After all, digging through different sources, one can find that Country is an English dance brought to America by immigrants.

A little later, I found information about *"Square dance"*, which in many states of America has the official status of a folk dance. Each square in the dance is formed by four pairs, facing each other. The peculiarity is that the sequence of figures performed in the dance is not known in advance. They are pronounced or sung by a caller. He leads the dance, but does not participate in it himself.

The style of clothing does not imply special costumes for this dance. But, quite often, you can find men wearing shirts with long sleeves, cowboy hats and boots. And women in bright dresses with wide skirts, under which multi-layered underskirts are worn.

Here I would like to make a note and once again draw your attention to the fact that I am still in search and study of American Nation Culture.

Summing up the review of several folk dances of different countries, it is clear how different all the people of our planet are, how different the mentality and culture. And the dances of the nations of the world are just an immense and incredibly interesting sphere of study.

3.3 BUILDING A FOLK DANCE LESSON

In this section, I would like you to recall the exercise of classical dance. Earlier, I mentioned that in my life there was quite a lot of ballet dance. So we talked about the fact that the folk dance, as we see it today, has absorbed the basis of classical choreography for a reason.

The entire structure of the lesson can be conditionally divided into 3 integral parts: warm-up; jumps and virtuoso technique; and dances of different world nationalities.

Warm-up:

So, the first experience and acquaintance with folk choreography takes place in exactly the same way as in ballet choreography – with the rhythmic for the smallest students, the acquaintance with the music and its perception of tempo-rhythms, as well as a mandatory parterre warm-up or stretching.

In older groups of students, the warm-up takes place in the key of classical exercise near the ballet barre, performing all the designated movements from plie to grand battement in their classical forms. Also, this type of warm-up can be transferred to the middle of the dance hall. Why the ballet warm-up is used in the folk choreography... Everything is easy. Why do we need to reinvent the wheel if we already have exercises that develop all muscle groups and involve all the necessary components of the body.

But the most interesting thing happens at the next level of the age group. Here, the ballet warm-up becomes the dance near the choreographic barre. Since we are talking about folk dance, and there are lots of nationalities and characters of performance. It is necessary to introduce them to the students, but hardly a boy or a girl who came to dance lessons would listen a lecture. At least it's boring, at most it may not be quite clear in theory. Therefore, the movements of ballet dance exercise begin to be framed by certain nationalities and use the appropriate musical accompaniment of the chosen country. To make it clearer, I will give an example: The warm-up begins with demi and grand plie based on the Greek "folk" dance "Sirtaki" (written in quotes, because it is not quite right to call it folk). And then this mini dance becomes as diverse as the teacher's imagination allows. You can go into grand plie and make a full turn at the bottom to change legs, you can use your hands as in the performance of the dance, you can add national dance movements and attitude and more. That is, while performing a given movement, you dance in a certain manner.

Warm-up based on Georgian folk dance "Kartuli".
Kyiv National University of Culture and Arts (2013).

The second part of the lesson **Jumps** and **Virtuoso Technique:**

Again, the rules of the jumping part are equated to the classical Allegro. Special characteristic movements based on the materials of world dances can also be added. Example: Renverse Jump in the character of the gypsy dance and what not.

With Virtuoso Technique, it's a bit more complicated: in some cases, the mechanisms of technique begin to be studied at the end of the exercise at the dance barre; in other cases – some elementary forms of performance are studied in the middle of the dance hall. Everything depends on the specific movement, and there are lots of them. Technical elements can be in the air (an example is the Ukrainian split), which contributes to the development of the so-called balloon (height of the jump) and split. Or some of the elements can be conducted down on the ground (barrel, crawler); or at the level of students' heights (fouette, all kinds of turns).

Virtuoso technique plays a huge role in folk dance, because (in most cases) it is that part which reflects the color and character of the dances of different nationalities of the world.

Georgia virtuoso technique.   Ukrainian type of turns – obertas.

Dances of Different Nationalities of the World:

This is the main and final part of the lesson in folk choreography. Here, the folk dance is studied and practiced, including its elements and performance characteristics. Interestingly, in most cases, folk choreography describes a story or depicts a plot. Performers play roles on the stage without verbal accompaniment.

For younger learners, this could be a dance game based on any nationality and their traditional games. Older performers may encounter more instructive or romantic story. Additionally, historical events of countries can be represented through folk dances.

Folk Choreographic Dance Ensemble "Friendship", Cherkasy city, Ukraine.
Beginners Dances.

3.4 APPEARANCE OF PERFORMERS IN FOLK CHOREOGRAPHY

My first experience in folk dance classes (1998).

Since folk dance incorporates elements of ballet dance, the appearance of dancers should be the same. For females, this includes a leotard, a dance bodysuit or a dance swimsuit; leggings or a chiton; ballet shoes (which are replaced with the hard shoes, which are folk shoes or shoes for folk dance. But they are worn by more experienced students during the second part of the lesson). For males, dance suit includes leggings or tight comfortable pants, a light tight-fitting T-shirt, and soft dance shoes or ballet shoes (which are replaced with dance boots or dance hard shoes in the second part of the lesson).

Folk shoes for females.

Folk shoes for males.

Quite often, in folk dance groups, you can find a dance uniform with the logo of the dance school to which the dancers belong. This is largely due to the huge number of participants of constant concerts, tournaments, competitions, and festivals in different cities or countries, where dancers represent the culture of their country or support another country by performing their folk dance.

It is important to remember that the stage costume differs from the dance uniform. It must correspond to the established samples of national clothing of the represented country, as well as align with the ideological and figurative content of the dance.

In addition to everything mentioned above, I want to add that folk dance, like any other dance, strives to keep up with the times. This is facilitated by the new generation of people and the new type of folk dance, which is now actively developing – "stylization of folk dance". It implies the infusion of folk choreography with the other types or styles of dance. I am a huge supporter of the stylization of folk choreography. After all, folk dance is designed to show the history and culture of each nationality. And what could better reflect history than all the new findings which we have nowadays. Because in 10-50 years our today's modern styled dance will become a history. The main requirement is not to overdo the styling and not to eradicate the "folk" essence from the dance.

4 BALLROOM DANCE

Nowadays, ballroom dance occupies a significant part of my life, as it is the type of choreography I am currently working with. In my opinion, ballroom dance is full of surprises. Throughout my work with this choreography, I changed my point of view about it quite often, sometimes for worse, and then for better.

It's worth noting that my choreography knowledge is extensive. For a long period of time, I was holding the position of Chief Choreographer of the Philharmonic in Ukraine, where I was working on innovative forms and stylizations in folk dance. I made a significant progress, leaving behind many beautiful choreographic productions that continue to be performed nowadays. Additionally, I worked as a guest choreographer in various theaters and dance studios, where a large part of my work was occupied by modern and ballroom choreography. Working quite a lot with this kind of dance, why only here, in the USA, I have contradictive feelings regarding ballroom dance? Why am I changing my opinion about it so often?

In the USA, my choreographic activity in ballroom dance began with teaching children (in Ukraine I had mostly worked with professionals). Here, I encountered the first obstacle on my path. All the coaches of this type of dance taught in their own way. Everyone had his/her own nuances. For me, this was unclear. Because, in every other type of dance, these nuances are important. One of them is structure, which has a principal meaning! But not here. I believe the following example will clarify what I am talking about. We know that the Triple Step in Jive has accents on 2,4,6,8; these are the accents in the music when the knee of the working leg should rise as high as possible. And here is my indignation when somebody skips one of the accents, and the other teacher adds an extra accent to the number 1, arguing that it is easier to teach this way. Or, another example, the Lock Step in the Cha-Cha-Cha dance. This is a step with an accent on the so-called step change in the Latin Cross Position. And what do we have here? Someone places the main foot a little forward with the step change and simultaneously making one extra step, meanwhile another teacher does this step change on the spot, without adding an extra step.

Unexpectedly, I discovered a problem: there is no structure in ballroom dance. There is no basic methodology for studying the material. The question is: Why does this happen and why does no one notice it? Is it because all teaching methods are correct? Is it because at a fast pace this is not noticeable? Is it because not all the ballroom dance teachers conducting professional development? I mean, was their coach enough for them, and they decided that it was the only correct way of teaching?

I suggest we start from the history of the formation of ballroom dance.

4.1 THE HISTORY OF THE FORMATION OF BALLROOM DANCE

Let's recall the branching that occurred during the formation of ballet dance. When the dance moved from the squares to the halls of the palaces, it began to divide society into "poor" and "rich". In the 18th century, the Waltz, Quadrille, Minuet, and Bolero were born. The elegance of manners, the nobility of posture, and the exquisite respectfulness from the peasants. That is, the "social dance" for the privileged is the progenitor of ballroom dance, which we know now.

Ballroom dance has absorbed not only the "elite dances" of those times but also part of folk dances. For example, Tango – the folk color of Argentina, which has taken its individual place in ballroom dance. Foxtrot can be attributed to the USA, which was inspired by Afro-American rhythms. Cha-Cha-Cha is filled with the exoticism and energy of Cubans. Pasodoble has Spanish roots, etc.

Ballroom dance formed and took its place in the world between the 19th and

20th centuries. Is it correct to say that ballroom dance is native in Europe?

Partially... Because it was precisely the Latin American and African musical and choreographic cultures of the 19th-20th centuries that gave "life" to ballroom choreography. These "roots" are well disguised so technically, that it becomes difficult to get to them.

The Golden age of ballroom dances is considered to be the period of the 1920s-1930s. Ballroom dance was actively developing all over the world. One of the driving factors that contributed to the flourishing of ballroom dance was the influence of the film industry and Broadway musicals. This century was also characterized by freedom and self-expression. Dancers could add improvisation to their performances, which added emotionality, while maintaining grace and elegance. At the same time, English experts standardized all known ballroom dances. Since then, ballroom dances has been divided into two directions: social and sport. Nowadays it is European and Latin American programs.

The European Program (Standard) includes:

1.   **Slow (English) Waltz**: The predecessor of this dance was the Boston Waltz from the USA (1874), but it only became fashionable in 1922.

2.   **Tango**: Originally from Argentina, this dance has evolved in several stages. First, the Polka rhythm was replaced by the Habanera rhythm. Later on, the original name "Baile con Corte" changed, and this dance became known as "Tango". The dance gained its popularity in Paris, where it underwent many trials and protests. French bishops, for example, pointed to its sexual character.

3.   **Slow Foxtrot**: This dance appeared much earlier than the Waltz and has been constantly improving. In 1919, an American named Thomas Hunt Morgan demonstrated an open spin-turn, which is now actively used in this dance. In 1920, the couple Ms. Josephine Bradley and Mr. G. K. Anderson added new dance figures, such as the feather step and change of direction. From 1922, the dance was performed on demi-pointes. Later on, Mr. Frank Ford introduced heel turns to the Foxtrot.

4.   **Viennese Waltz**: The first known melody of the Viennese Waltz is dated back to 1770. In 1813, Lord George Gordon Byron condemned this kind of Waltz for its impracticality and licentious character. In 1816, a similar reaction came from English high society. Such a struggle continued until 1833.

5.   **Quick Step**: In the 1920s, the Slow Foxtrot was played too fast. People started talking about the Fast Foxtrot. Of course, Charleston also played its role in the formation of this dance, which we all know as Quick Step.

The Latin American Program (Latin) includes:

1.   **Samba**: This dance came from Africa but it was adapted in Brazil. There are several types of Samba dance – from Baion to Marcha, performed at the carnival in Rio de Janeiro.

2.   **Cha-Cha-Cha**: Relatively new in the Latin American program, this dance was noticed in the 1950s at the dance halls of America. It originated from the Mambo dance, but the music became slower, and the rhythm was changed to less complex.

3.   **Rumba**: The most classic dance of the entire Latin American program. This dance contains elements of "tease and run". Which means to seduce a man, and then reject him.

4.   **Pasodoble**: A Spanish dance that was discovered in Mexico. A man represents a bullfighter, and a woman can play the role of a bull, or "sarra", which is a red bullfighter's cloak. The dance became popular around 1920.

5.   **Jive**: A swing dance that became fashionable in the 1940s. Its development was influenced by boogie-woogie, rock and roll, and American swing.

Originally, ballroom dance was considered to be a pair dance only. The pair consisted of a lady and a gentleman, who had to follow all points of contact. Nowadays, at all possible ballroom dance tournaments, you can meet both pair dance performances and solo ones. And the contact in the pair is of a free form, depending on the idea of the choreographic image or choreographic color. In 1924, ballroom dances were included in the program of the Olympic Games, which gave them the status of an official sport.

With all the above mentioned, it becomes clear that structuring a ballroom dance is quite difficult. It is as difficult as to find the right way to perform a figure, which was an improvisation of one of the performers, and later on began to be used as one of the main elements of the dance.

Well, perhaps the next section of this book will to show us new nuances of ballroom choreography. It's high time to understand the basic initial steps of ballroom dance and its integral component – tournament.

4.2 BALLROOM DANCE LESSON AND BASIC INITIAL FIGURES

Ballroom dance groups are unique and they are divided primarily by the dancer's skills, not their ages. Thus, in a group lesson, there can be children of various age categories. It should be noted that in ballroom dance, individual or private lessons still play a key role. This allows the coach to focus on the routine (a set of dancing movements) of a specific pair or solo performer, providing more opportunities to work out certain figures and improve them.

A ballroom dance lesson, like any other type of dance, always begins with a warm-up to prepare all muscle groups for active work. The warm-up, however, is far from classical choreography. It more closely resembles a sport warm-up with music, starting from the head and cervical vertebrae and moving down to affect the shoulders, arms, torso, ending with the knees and feet.

After that the actual dance part of the lesson starts, where either new steps are studied, or the routine of a specific dance is practiced. It's worth saying that usually during a lesson, the group manages to work on only two, sometimes three dances of the ballroom program.

We know that there are two programs of ballroom dance, which include 10 different ballroom dances. The beginners study the basic steps and figures of these dances. Growing professionally, the dancer chooses one direction (Standard or Latin), over which he or she continues to work and improve.

The basic figures which build the foundation for performing routines at tournaments or competitions, and raise the level of the performer, include:

Square FWD/BWD

Three change FWD/BWD ⊢ Slow Waltz

Natural Turn (Big Square)

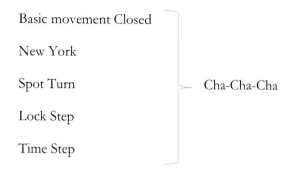

Basic movement Closed

New York

Spot Turn

Lock Step

Time Step

Cha-Cha-Cha

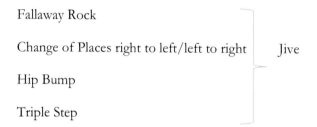

Fallaway Rock

Change of Places right to left/left to right

Hip Bump

Triple Step

Jive

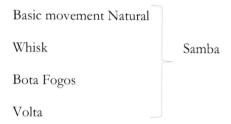

Basic movement Natural

Whisk

Bota Fogos

Volta

Samba

Basic Movement Closed

New York

Spot Turn

Time Step

Rumba

Of course, it should be added that there is no specific order of learning figures, and there is no quantity limit. Everything depends on the individual abilities of the student and the creativity of the teacher. This list of initial steps can increase.

Also, you may have noticed the same names of steps in different dances. This is not a mistake! The names are not only the same, these steps have, practically, the same figures. The distinguishing feature is their performance, different count of musical layout, different tempo rhythms, and modified presentation. Although the basis remains the same.

4.3 BALLROOM DANCE COMPETITIONS

Ballroom dances are often associated with sports because the primary goal of every ballroom dancer is the participation in competitions and championships. The dancers aim to represent themselves and their country by receiving medals, cups, and titles such as Candidate Master of Sports and/or Master of Sports.

In the dance world, ballroom choreography tournaments are divided into three programs: European (Standard), Latin American (Latin), and Ten-Dance (dancers who perform both programs).

There are amateur competitions (IDSF), where the dancers of all the levels can participate. There are also professional competitions, which confer titles and recognitions. The most prestigious competitions remain "UK Open" and "Blackpool Dance Festival". In the USA, participation in "Pro-Am" tournaments is very popular. "Pro-Am" stands for Professional-Amateur, where a coach (professional) can pair with a student (amateur), thereby relieving stress from the participants and assisting them counting musical size, its accents, and the correct sequential execution of dance figures.

In America, "American Smooth" and "American Rhythm" competitions are very popular. "American Smooth" is a variation of the European program, but it includes only four dances instead of five: Waltz, Tango, Foxtrot, and Viennese Waltz. It also differs from European dances of the International program by the free position of partners, which allows a room for improvisation. "American Rhythm" is a variation of the Latin American program, which includes five dances: Cha-Cha-Cha, Rumba, Swing, Bolero, and Mambo. The difference with the Latin American program is evident in the composition of the dances.

It should be noted that all amateur competitions are divided not only by the age of the participants (children; juveniles; juniors; youth; adults; seniors and grand-seniors), but also by their level (beginner – bronze; silver; gold; which are further divided into categories). Thus, anyone who wishes can participate in the competition.

Competitions, in turn, are divided into two types:

1.   Singles – where each selected and performed dance (among 10 of them) is evaluated separately;

2.   Multi (Challenge) – where one score is given for the selected and performed dance package on the floor.

Remember, at the very beginning of the book, I mentioned that ballroom choreography was not affordable for my family. So, in addition to the monthly payments for classes and payments for private lessons (optional), one has to purchase dance uniform and shoes, also competition costumes, and pay for hairstyle, makeup, etc., while you need to pay for the competitions as well. The cost of which usually includes an entrance ticket for the participant and the coach, contributions or late registration fees, payment to the coach (not always), and payment for each selected dance or dance package.

4.4 APPEARANCE OF BALLROOM DANCERS

If we are talking about rehearsals, then it is important that the clothes are comfortable and do not restrict movements. For the European program, classic clothes in basic colors are suitable. For women – dresses, tunics, pants and midi/maxi skirts, as well as closed hills for the "Standard". For men – shirts, polo shirts, pants and shoes (Standard).

Examples of dance uniform for the European Program (Standard).

Latin allows you to dress brightly and creatively. Women: stretch dresses, leggings, pareos, mini-skirts, tops and open hills for the Latin American program. Men: sports pants or stretch pants (dance pants), tank tops, T-shirts, shirts and Latin shoes.

Examples of dance uniform for the Latin American Program.

There is such a concept as a competition look. This is not only a costume, but also accessories, hairstyle, and makeup.

The competition costume should suit this particular dancer, emphasize the character of his/her movements, hide flaws and focus attention on the charm of the figure, be as comfortable as possible, and make the dancer noticeable on the floor. If you have a pair tournament – it is important that the costumes of the partners look harmonious.

Men's should only have black socks, girls should have white socks or sheer tights. It is unacceptable for underwear to peek out from under a bodysuit or a dress. All jewelry should perfectly match the costume.

Men need a quality hairdo just as much as girls do. It is recommended to use special products that will not allow the hairstyle to get disheveled during dances. Makeup should consist of rich colors that will make the face expressive.

It is noteworthy that for mistakes in costumes, tournament judges can deduct points. It is important to remember that appearance is 30 percent of success on the floor. And each age category has its own ruleset in competition appearance.

5 MODERN DANCE AND ITS HISTORY

Surprisingly, modern dance also originates from classical/ballet dance. Its history of emergence is usually traced back to the 19th-20th centuries. It arose in the directions of free movement, modern dance, and expressive dance, as a result of society's reaction to the strict and firm rules of ballet dance. This time can be classified as a "search for freedom".

Of course, the most famous representative of free dance was Isadora Duncan. Her unique stage style (dancing barefoot, dancing what she felt) amazed and delighted the audience.

The founder of the expressive dance was the German - Mary Wigman, who was one of the first to reject dance movements, which were traditionally considered beautiful.

Isadora Duncan (1877-1927).
Pic was taken from Wikipedia.
She was an American dancer and a choreographer.
Isadora plated a pivotal role in liberating ballet from its conservative constraints and paved the way for expressive dance.

Mary Wigman (1886-1973).
Pic was taken from Wikipedia.
She was a German dancer and a choreographer, notable as the pioneer of expressionist dance, dance therapy, and movement training without pointe shoes.

In the first half of the 1930s, modern ideas were refined in the USA, Germany, and Western Europe. In the 1920s, the Bauhaus Dance Theater appeared in Germany, which was an experimental center. It brought together artists, designers, and choreographers who created unique dance compositions. Starting from the second half of the same year, the USA became the center of the development of modern dance. In the 1930s, Marta Graham opened the dance school in America. Her technique was based on the use of body weight and expressive movements. She developed the "contraction and release" technique, which means "the movement is subject to breathing".

Marta Graham (1894-1991).
Pic was taken from Wikipedia.
She was an influential American dancer, a teacher, and a choreographer of modern dance. Her ballets and other works were intended to "reveal the inner man". Over more than 50 years, she created more than 180 works, from solo to large-scale productions, often performing in them herself. Graham's intense and forceful expression of primal emotions gave modern dance new depth.

Simultaneously with modern dance, jazz dance was refined in the 1970s. During that period, various styles and techniques of dance were combined into one. Choreographers actively began to use contact dance and improvisation. And as a result, new directions of dance appeared: modern, jazz-modern, contemporary. Later on, hip-hop culture was created, the components of which were rap, breakdance, graffiti, street types of dance.

Despite the fact that hip-hop was originated a long time ago in various corners of North America, its homeland is considered to be the South Bronx (New York). People without professional training, but with a great desire to dance, brought those dances to the city streets. Here a logical question arises: Can hip-hop dance culture be attributed to national, or folk dances of America? In my subjective opinion, the answer will be "YES". If we return again to the history of the formation of folk dance, its creation will be basically the same as the history of hip-hop culture.

Today, hip-hop is divided into many components. Old school: hip-hop, breakdance, krump, flexing, C-Walk, Turfing, Locking and Popping (Funk Styles). New school (New styles): elements of Old school directions, pop culture, reggae, modern, Latin and Belly dances.

Thus, the history of the creation and development of modern dance is a history of experiments and innovations that have led to the creation of a large number of unique and emotional dance directions.

5.1 BUILDING A MODERN CHOREOGRAPHY DANCE LESSON

Warm-up: Of course, the warm-up will depend on the chosen direction of modern dance. If we are talking about modern dance or contemporary – the warm-up will be very similar to the echoes of ballet dance. This can be the same exercise, which we are already familiar with, but with twisted positions and postures, contradictory to classical dance. Sometimes the warm-up can be in the pure form of ballet choreography.

If, however, we are talking about hip-hop or breakdance – then, most likely, the warm-up will be closer to sports, like the warm-up in ballroom choreography.

In the dance itself, the same tendency is preserved as in the warm-up. Hip-hop is more about improvisation (freestyle) and emotions. There can be no strict school of dance, everyone dances as they feel. Each dancer develops his or her own style based on basic moves, such as bounce, modern steps, kicks, rocks; movements like Snake, Chicken-head, Cabbage Patch, Running man and much more. But the main element of the dance always remains the bounce (groove).

To master the art of Modern, Jazz-Modern or Contemporary dance, performers must fully control their bodies, jump, have good stretch (splits), plasticity, and coordination. Improvisations also take place here. These dances are built according to classic dance, often have a plot line or remake classical ballets in their modern style.

5.2 APPEARANCE OF A DANCER IN A MODERN DIRECTION

In modern dance, there are no strict rules for the appearance of a dancer. T-shirts, sports pants, shorts, sneakers, jazz shoes are acceptable. The main requirement is comfortable clothing. So that nothing interferes with jumping, turning, and squatting.

However, for individual modern dance styles, a special uniform may be applicable. For example, the High Heels direction requires dancing in high-heeled shoes; Contemporary – in soft shoes or even barefoot. Hip-Hop implies a street style, where one can use headgear, such as bandanas, baseball caps, caps. Jazz Funk welcomes an extravagant style with a bright combination of colors. Reggaeton and Dancehall prefer clothing that emphasizes the line of the hips and buttocks.

Whatever it is, but the most attention should be paid to the shoes.

Dance Jazz Shoes.

Dance Sneakers.

CONCLUSION

I tried to write this book as straightforwardly as possible, incorporating examples and pictures which, I believe, render the information more comprehensible. While not all the knowledge I possess is included in here, I deemed it unnecessary. My objective is to showcase the diversity of the dance world and the unique aspects of each choreographic style.

I trust that upon reading this material, you will concur that choreography is a splendid art which enables one to experience a wide spectrum of feelings and emotions. Everybody who has ever danced could consider themselves fortunate. From the moment they engaged with dance, they began to perceive the world around them aesthetically, cultivating a refined taste and style.

Thus, at this juncture, you can regard yourself as an enlightened individual in the realm of dance art.

At this point we are close to what I consider to be the most crucial part of this book. As we have already learned how to distinguish and understand each type of dance, several questions arise: Where should one commence their study of choreography? How does one choose a dance style? How can one find a suitable dance school? How does one select a dance instructor? These are the questions we will explore right now.

CHOOSING A DANCE STYLE

The initial step in your journey of choreography studying will be selection of a dance style that best suits you and resonates with your interests. Taking into consideration all the above-mentioned information, I anticipate that you will manage it easily.

It's crucial to complete a list of your goals and expectations. If you're seeking a dance school for you child, you'll need to create two lists: one is yours (describing parent's expectations) and another one belongs to your child (it's better when your kid will tell you all the goals and you will only write them down without judging). Ask yourself and you child, "What are my objectives? What do I hope to gain from dance classes?" For adults, this could encompass a variety of aspects, such as improving posture, participating in competitions, or boosting self-esteem. For children, the focus might be on having fun, socializing, or making new friends. Aim to write sincerely and list at least 10 points.

With these lists in hand, you'll get a clearer overall picture. As a parent, your next step is to align each of your and your child's point with the appropriate dance style, based on the information you've gathered from this book.

For instance:

- Improving posture – Classical dance/Ballet
- Competitions – Ballroom dance or Modern dance
- Increasing self-esteem – Classical dance/Ballet or Ballroom dance
- Having fun – Folk dance or Modern dance

Upon completing this task, you'll identify which dance style or styles align with your goals and meet your expectations.

Among these choreographic styles, consider your preferences and physical capabilities. Validate your choice or your child's choice by researching reviews of dances in the chosen style, attending some concerts, or watching tournaments to experience the dance firsthand.

AI Picture – Ballet Dance.

AI Picture – Ballroom Dance.

AI Picture – Folk Dance.

AI Picture – Modern Dance.

HOW TO FIND A DANCE SCHOOL AND CHOOSE AN INSTRUCTOR

Once you've chosen a dance style, the following step is to locate a dance school that specializes in your chosen choreography. Seek out a school with a solid reputation and qualified instructors. It's worth noting that the nearest dance school to your home may not always be the best choice. I recommend perusing the dance school's websites, where you'll typically find information about the dance instructors, their education, experience, and accomplishments. Reading reviews and comments about the school from others can also be insightful, and you may come across specific feedback about the school's teachers.

The next step involves signing up to visit the dance studio. It would be beneficial to observe a portion of a dance lesson for the age category you're interested in. This will allow you to familiarize yourself with the teaching style of a particular instructor and determine whether their approach to teaching aligns with your or your child's learning style. Consider whether a disciplined or playful method of presenting choreographic information is important to your child, and whether he/she values consistent self-improvement or occasional diversions to jokes, games, or other activities that lighten the mood.

When choosing a dance teacher, remember the cardinal rule - a dance teacher should nurture the individuality of each unique student. The execution of each choreographic idea in dance should be dependent on the skills and abilities of the students.

It's also worth noting that a good dancer may not necessarily make a good teacher, just as a good teacher may not always be a good dancer. Being a dance teacher is a calling. It requires someone who is rich in choreographic knowledge and can present this information easily and accurately. I've encountered a remarkable dance teacher whose appearance didn't fit the conventional image of a "professional dancer". However, he possessed a natural talent for teaching students, and many of them went on to receive "Honored" titles. Conversely, I've worked with the current performers of dance art who, while being inspiring and delightful in their dance, unfortunately lacked the ability to teach students.

Choosing an instructor is an entirely personal decision. It's challenging to recommend someone as each dance teacher has their own methodology, and what suits one person may not suit another. That's why I recommend trying classes with a specific teacher for yourself. You may need to explore several different dance schools, or perhaps try studying with different instructors within your chosen dance school.

Thanks to modern conveniences, you can often try the first lesson for free or for a minimal fee. Studying choreography can be an exhilarating and creative process, opening up new avenues for self-expression and development. By following my recommendations for choosing a dance style, selecting a dance school, and an instructor, you'll be well-equipped to master this art and achieve your goals.

QUESTIONS AND ANSWERS:

1. — *How long does it take to learn a dance?*
   - The duration needed for learning a specific dance varies greatly, depending on the individual abilities of a student, his/her prior experience, and the level of commitment to the learning process.

2. — *Should a dance teacher have a choreographic education?*
   - While having a formal education is always beneficial for a teacher, there can be exceptions. Some individuals are naturally gifted dance teachers, even without formal education. In this profession, experience, practice, and a creative approach are equally important.

3. — *What qualities should a dance instructor possess?*
   - A dance instructor should have solid foundation in the field of choreography. They should understand how specific movements impact the body and muscles. Additionally, the instructor should be capable of structuring the learning material in a manner that safeguards the student's health. Key qualities include creative thinking, good musicality, a sense of rhythm, the ability to work with people, as well as patience and perseverance.

4. — *Can choreography be studied without professional school or instructor?*
   - Absolutely. The art of dance can be studied independently using video lessons, books, and other resources. However, keep in mind that not all the material available on internet platforms will be of high quality and

professionalism. Working with an instructor, in contrast, can significantly accelerate your progress and help avoid common mistakes.

5. — *What should I do if I can't choose a dance style?*
   - If you're struggling to decide on a dance style, consider attending different classes or master-classes across various genres. This will help you understand which style of dance you enjoy. You can also seek advice from a dance teacher or professional dancer.

6. — *Why does my dance instructor insist on memory training?*
   - Memorizing and sequentially performing dance movements is a crucial aspect of choreography. Train regularly your memory by repeating educational dance elements. Work on your coordination, especially if the dance style you have chosen involves complex and fast movements.

7. — *Why is stretching needed in dances?*

   - Stretching is a fundamental skill for every dancer. Be prepared to dedicate time to exercises that develop flexibility, strength, coordination, and musicality. Patience and perseverance are key factors during the early stages of studying choreography.

INTERESTING FACTS ABOUT CHOREOGRAPHY:

- Dance classes can burn a significant number of calories.
- Ballet performances can be as physically demanding as a 30-kilometer run or two football matches.
- Choreography enhances peripheral vision, as dancers must be aware of their surroundings without turning their heads.
- Dance rehearsals foster endurance akin to that of athletes.
- Most artists in the dance genre retire between the ages of 30 and 35, with some continuing until 50.
- Despite the short career span, artists can achieve public recognition and win prestigious titles in this field.
- The first performance on the stage with a new dance is referred to as a "Premiere".
- Dancing can improve memory and physical activity.
- In the 1830s, the Can-Can was predominantly danced by men.
- Jean-Claude Van Damme, who studied ballet in his youth, ones stated, "If you can survive a ballet workout, you can survive a workout in any sport".
- Breakdance is included in the Olympic Games program.
- The term "Breakdancing" was coined by journalists to make the origin name "Breaking" more accessible to the general public.
- Dance therapy is recognized as a form of psychotherapy.
- Dance serves as a non-verbal language of communication.
- In Strasbourg in 1518, a dance epidemic known as "Dance Fever or Dancing Mania" occurred, where hundreds of townspeople danced non-stop for several days.
- Dancing can control the lipid levels, resulting in an increase in "good" cholesterol and a decrease in "bad" cholesterol in the blood.
- Dancing can help to prevent injuries in everyday life.
- Dancing is considered a remedy for anxiety.
- The world record for the longest Conga dance chain was set in Miami in 1988 by a group of 119,986 people.

- The dance "Capoeira" was invented 300-400 years ago by African slaves in Brazil, who were prohibited from practicing fight arts. They ingeniously combined dances with fights.
- Ballerinas typically go through 2-3 pairs of pointe shoes per week.
- A single ballet pack for a ballerina takes approximately 75 hours to create.
- Dance became recognized as a crucial element of pop music largely due to Michael Jackson.
- The Guinness Book of Records still holds the unbeaten record of an Indian dancer for the longest dance, which lasted 123 hours and 15 minutes.
- In the Chinese dance "Dance of a Thousand Hands", 21 female dancers participate, but the audience perceives only one. The rest are concealed behind her, creating the illusion of a multi-armed woman dancing.
- April 29 is celebrated as International Dance Day, established by UNESCO in 1982.

ABOUT THE AUTHOR

Anastasiia Ohirchuk graced the world on December 8th, 1992, in the vibrant city of Cherkasy in Ukraine. From her very first breath, she carried within her an innate love for movement – a rhythm that would shape her destiny. As a child, Anastasiia twirled non-stop in the small cozy apartment in Cherkasy, her tiny feet barely grazing the floor. Her parents watched her dancing with the admiration, their hearts attuned to the music of her spirit. Recognized their daughter's fervor, Anastasiia's parents enrolled her in the dance classes at the tender age of four. The studio became her sanctuary – a sacred space where music and motion merged into something magical. Here, she learned not only the steps but also the language of expression. The wooden floors absorbed her dreams, and the mirrors reflected her determination.

At fourteen, Anastasiia's talent blossomed further. She joined a Semi-Professional Folk Dance team, where her graceful movements earned her more than applauses – they brought her first salaries. The stage became her canvas, and the spotlight was her brush.

High school graduation marked a pivotal moment. Anastasiia set her sights on Kyiv National University of Culture and Arts. Fate, however, played a whimsical tune during her creative competition. The music faltered, but Anastasiia didn't miss a beat. She not only danced but also sang, her voice produced melodies that resonated through the auditorium. She impressed the judging committee with her great desire and persistence, and the university doors swung open, so she could step into her desired path.

In 2015, Anastasiia earned her Bachelor's Degree, her passion for dance fueling her academic journey. But her hunger for knowledge didn't wane. In 2017, she proudly donned her Master's Degree in Choreography. During this period of time, she wrote her first research paper, titled "Theatre Directing Aspects of Ballet Master Activity in Folk Choreography". This article was presented at the All-Ukrainian Scientific and Practical Conference in 2016, which was published in the book "Choreography of the 21st Century: Artistic and Educational Potential".

Simultaneously, Anastasiia was working as a guest Choreographer at the Dnipropetrovsk Youth Theater and the Kamianske Theater named after Lesia Ukrainka. Her choreography graced stages across Ukraine and beyond, leaving audiences spellbound.

In 2017, she ascended to become the youngest Chief Choreographer of the

Philharmonic in Ukraine. Over fifty choreographic performances bore her signature. She is an innovator, introducing new forms of expression to the Philharmonic stage in Ukraine.

In 2018, Anastasiia's expertise extended to performative and stage arts at the Ukrainian Cultural Foundation. Her insights enriched the cultural landscape, bridging traditions and innovations.

In 2022, Anastasiia's family migrated to America due to the war in Ukraine. The new home embraced her, and her passion for dance continued to flourish.

Anastasiia's hunger for knowledge knew no bounds. Driven by an insatiable curiosity, she sought to elevate her qualifications. Her journey led her to prestigious institutions. At Harvard University, she immersed herself in the course "Stravinsky's Rite of Spring: Modernism, Ballet, and Riots". The rhythms on Stravinsky's masterpiece resonated with her soul, infusing her choreography with newfound depth. Emory University welcomed her for the course "So You Think You Know Tango". There, she explored the passionate embrace of this sultry dance form, unraveling its secrets step by step.

In 2023, Anastasiia embarked on a mission – to ignite the spark of dance in young hearts across the USA. Her experiences, wisdom, and love for movement culminated in the release of her book "What do you know about dance?".

Anastasiia Ohirchuk's career continued to develop and became a beacon for aspiring dancers and curious souls.

ABOUT THOSE WHO INFLUENCED ANASTASIIA'S CHOREOGRAPHIC THINKING

Anastasiia (second person from the left) and Radu Poklitary (next to Anastasiia). Attending Radu's modern ballet "The Nutcracker and the Mouse King", 2012.

Radu Poklitaru – the founder and the Chief Ballet Master of the Kyiv Modern-Ballet Academic Theatre. Professor of the Department of Modern Choreography at the Kyiv National University of Culture and Arts. The Honored Worker of Culture of Ukraine. The winner of Shevchenko National Prize of Ukraine. The winner of the Personality of the Year Prize. The People's Artist of Moldova. The laureate of numerous international contests.

Larysa Tsvetkova (in the center of the picture) with her students during ballet class at Kyiv National University of Culture and Arts, 2013.

Larysa Tsvetkova – Honored Worker of Culture of Ukraine, Associate Professor. The author of the textbook "Methodology of teaching ballet dance". She has numerous programs and methodological recommendations on choreographic disciplines for higher education institutions of Ukraine. She has repeatedly presented her pedagogical achievements at seminars, workshops of various levels for teachers-choreographers in Ukraine and abroad. Larysa Tsvetkova is a permanent member of the jury of All-Ukrainian festival of folk dance competition named after Pavlo Virsky, and international festival competition of the national dances of the world "Rainbow Terpsichora".

Larysa Tsvetkova (in the center of the picture). Anastasiia (person from the right). Bachelor's Degree, 2015.

Anastasiia Ohirchuk, 2011.
Kyiv National University of Culture and Arts.
Modern Dance Lesson.

Dear Readers,
May the pages you've turned in this book continue to resonate with rhythm and inspiration.
As you step beyond these words, may your own dance unfold – a choreography of dreams,
determination, and joy. Keep moving, keep believing, and may your journey be as graceful as
a pirouette.

With heartfelt wishes,
Anastasiia Ohirchuk

ANASTASIIAOGIRCHUK

Made in the USA
Columbia, SC
01 July 2024

6c5aa911-246b-4cc7-9c23-ffac83837501R01